The Book on Ca

MW00944891

The Prof's Guide to Graduating with a Job Offer

Second in a series on College & Career Readiness

By: Lisa Vento Nielsen, MBA, PMP

Founder, The Next Step

www.thenextstep1234.com

College and Career Readiness Seminar Guru

Dedicated to my children Sofia and Christopher Nielsen

Table of Contents

Introduction

This installment of the College and Career Readiness series is focused on career readiness and graduating with a job offer.

I have spent so much time over the last 13 years as an educator focusing on getting my students ready for the real world in addition to teaching them the subject matter at hand that putting these lessons into a book is the best way to share it with everyone who is interested in being ready after graduation to begin their CAREER.

I use the word CAREER instead of JOB for a reason. People can focus on getting a job but the best thing you can do is to think in terms of career. The economy and the skill sets are changing so rapidly but there are ways to be more prepared and more "hirable" than your competition and reading this book is the way to do it.

I will discuss and provide actionable lessons on the following topics that you can then apply to your life and help you to be ready to graduate with a job offer and then you can read my Entrepreneur-ING series to continue to be the boss of your own career:

Chapter 1: Completing Your Degree with "Distinction"

This chapter will discuss how to stand out amongst others graduating with you across the nation. I will discuss what graduating with "distinction" means and how you can leverage this for your career search. If you read the first installment of this series, you should know what skills you needed to work on and how to make them visible to the world. If not, I will provide all of the quick ways you can achieve distinction at the 11th hour before graduation and during interviewing season.

Chapter 2: Building On Those Networks

This chapter will discuss the best ways to build your network and how to get noticed for the right reasons. We will discuss making the most out of your school work and your school to help you get on the right road to making contacts and having interviews.

Chapter 3: How to Write the Perfect Resume

With over 15 years of resume writing and hiring experience, I will show you the best methods to make the perfect resume applicable to all; I will also have a feedback look implemented where I will be open to receiving resumes for review, as part of the book.

Chapter 4: How to Write Your Cover Letters to Get Noticed

The cover letter is wrongly considered unnecessary; it is necessary and it must be written in an engaging and intriguing way to get you into the door for the opportunities that are out there. This chapter is full of templates and writing ideas to make your cover letter stand out from the crowd.

Chapter 5: Using LinkedIn and Other Social Media to Stand Out for the Right Reasons

Many jobs today are not listed publicly but instead are filled via social media and LinkedIn. Having an awesome LinkedIn profile is a necessity to finding your place in the world and I will walk you through my proprietary 14-step guide to improving your profile and give you for free my lessons on how to use your new profile to stand out for the right reasons. This will also apply to other social media platforms.

Chapter 6: On Interviewing

My hacks and tips on how to be prepared for interviewing. I will discuss the different interview styles, methods and formulations in terms of how you are asked questions, where and the amount of interviewers.

Chapter 7: Interviewing Skills for In-Person Interviews

How to make a personable connection during interviews, how to act on the interview, what to say and how to say it and more.

Chapter 8: Media Training Overview

This is about something near and dear to my heart and that I do extensive training on in real life – how to manage interviews held via technology. There are rules and tips on how to make a connection via Skype or other technology.

Chapter 9: What to Do After the Interview

The full guide on what to do (and not to do) after the interview. I will include detailed information on thank you notes how to write them, why to write them and more.

Chapter 10: Finding Opportunities

More insights into how to take your next step; how to find a career path and what to do when you do not know what you want to do.

Chapter 11: Closing the Deal or Negotiating and Accepting the Offer

On negotiating salary, getting letters of recommendation that will help you get the job and starting on your first day.

Chapter 12: Building Your Career with Skills and Learning

Sneak peek at book "The Prof's Guide to Entrepreneur-ing: Using Entrepreneurial Skills to Launch Your Own Business or be the Boss of Your Career"

Chapter 1:

Completing Your Degree with Distinction

What does this chapter hope to be about? In a perfect world, you would have started college with the first book in this series, The Book on College Readiness - The Prof's Guide to Surviving High School and Kicking Butt in College and been ready and able to execute all of those tips and insights into your four years at college.

If you are reading this book and are still in college even if you are a junior or a young senior (meaning you still have at least a semester to go), it would behoove you to put this book down and go back to the first book in the series to see more about achieving success as a college student.

If you do not have time for that because the clock is ticking on your graduation walk and you really need to execute on finding a job and a potential career path forthwith, then let us just review together some ways for you to finish your degree with distinction.

In 2016, approximately 32% of Americans are going to college to get their degrees. That means that what was once a very unique thing to do is now much more common.

Many people are in the market right now with undergraduate degrees and there are also many people with advanced degrees, as well. There are people who went to better schools than you (maybe) and who got better grades than you (maybe) and were involved with more activities, had more work experience etc. – did I totally depress you yet?

There will always be someone who is "better" at certain things than you but there will never be another YOU and by reading and executing on the lessons in this book, you will stand out (for the right reasons) and beat your competition.

How do I know this? I know this based off of over 13 years' experience as an executive, educator and entrepreneur. I know this by being the person who sat waiting for a job interview with other grads from Harvard, Cornell and other Ivy League schools and still knowing I could beat them at anything because I had a more complete package and/or the confidence and/or the grit to get things done and be more competitive. And I knew that way back in 1998 before I had my years in as an executive, entrepreneur and educator.

This book will share with you the steps you can take and how to make sure you can be the most confident person in the room – not cocky, just confident. There is a large difference between confidence and arrogance. You are going to own the room with the skills and lessons I will give you in this book and with that you will be ready to graduate with a job offer.

Graduating with distinction really includes having been involved, having done the best you could in your academics while also having some work experience, internships, volunteer activities and more. It is not too late for all of this (so long as you have at least 3-6 months until graduation). I cannot help you boost your GPA magically in this amount of time but I can help you build out your resume and your skills to be ready for these interviews that will hopefully be scheduled. I will also help you identify how to find and set up interviews so you are not just waiting on the sidelines but are front and center for companies, hiring managers and more.

If you have any time whatsoever, begin to brainstorm on what you have done as an undergrad that warrants publicity. What things have you accomplished that you want to draw attention to for you to graduate with distinction. Did you work while attending school? Did you pay your own way without much help from home? Did you learn another language? Did you study abroad? (Please tell me you studied abroad – I am a huge proponent of getting out of your home country and exploring, learning and living in another culture. I got the opportunity at 21 to leave the country and it changed my life for the better in so many ways that I still experience the benefits of this now almost two decades later.)

Did you volunteer somewhere that meant something to you? Are you so unique that you actually created something like a business that you ran out of your dorm room? Or did a professor force you to do a project where you had to invent and market a new product and you hated doing it but now you have all of this great research, writing samples and a portfolio showcasing the entrepreneurial you.

As an educator since 2003, I have always made my classes present – I am the #profwhomakesyoupresent after all. Many of the projects have been focused on executing on a business plan, with financial templates to develop new product and service ideas. In doing this, I have found students to be so inspiring with great ideas really cutting edge to the point that I have suggested to many students to launch and/or patent their ideas.

Think if you have anything like this – consider starting something from your dorm room or from home if you are a commuting student. I have taught students who also were executing on products and/or running their own businesses on the side. One of them had a t-shirt business that was almost art-like in the t-shirts created and sold by him. As I continue to teach, more and more students are interested in considering entrepreneurial pursuits or having a "side-gig" to help with the expenses.

Include any and all work experience you have; if you do not have some and you have at least a semester left, get involved, get an internship or a volunteer opportunity something to add to your resume and make the distinction possible.

For many hiring manager, GPA is NOT the most important thing. Yes, I know that might come as a shock to you but for many people out there looking to fill the few positions that open up every year, across industries and even globally, the focus is not just on GPA. It is still "important" but not the main way to graduate with distinction.

The GPA should be at least a 3.0 if not in the whole cumulative sense then in the major. This will allow you to highlight it on your resume. It is important to at least have one GPA that is 3.0 or higher but it is not truly imperative to do what I suggest in terms of distinction.

Have the background and the experience to show you can tell stories and that you can motivate people (including yourself) when times get tough. Show you are wise beyond your years by making sure your social media profile is managed as a professional to be and not as a Kardashian to be. We will talk about this more in Chapter 5.

Be resilient and able to learn new skills quickly – have this be demonstrable in both your resumes, cover letters and your interviewing skills and styles – we will be covering these lessons and how-to's in chapters 3, 4 and 6.

These lessons I am sharing with you are information that I have been sharing and creating for the past 13 years as an educator. It is also information I have used as an executive in Corporate America and as an entrepreneur, too. These lessons have helped countless students and clients of mine graduate with a job offer and go on to successful careers.

I thank you for looking to me for your lessons on how to graduate with a job offer. You will find that the information I share is useful and applicable to your daily lives as you prepare for your next step into the world of a working adult.

This is one of the hardest times in history to get started on a career that can lead to long term benefits and growth. You will need to be flexible and consider alternate options in building your career. As I tell my students, this is one of the first times in history where you might not do better than your parents but a lot of this is due to the constant growth and the fact that many more people are going to college. So for me, I was the first in my family to complete a Bachelor's and a MBA degree but for you, many people might have received degrees in your family.

Many "older" people in their 50's, 60's and beyond are still working or involved with companies making there be less turnover with retirees aging out of the system and you and your colleagues jumping in to take over. I explain this in class that many people in their 50's and 60's are more youthful than ever before (and I speak from experience as my parents are in their late 50's/early 60's) this age group is not what it was like when I was a kid – these people are vibrant and have tons of experience.

This book will help you get past the age old problem of needing experience to get the job and needing the job to get experience. You will learn in this book tools and techniques to get ahead of the competition and get yourself that experience to build on a lifetime of career opportunity!

Chapter 2:

Building On Your Networks

The most important thing to think about as you prepare to graduate is your network. Who is part of your network? Do you have a network? Who can you rely on from family and friends to help you on your way to this big next step and at the same time, who can you help as you move forward.

I have said before in previous books that I am a big proponent of giving back and that doing for others can help when you are networking and looking for people to "do" for you. If you have this mentality of giving back and stepping up even if it is just by sharing information and/or connecting two people who can help each other in their businesses or life, this is all a great way to make sure that networking you do is a two way street and will be more fruitful because of it.

In the first installment of this book, The Book on College Readiness, I discuss in detail how to begin to build your network and now that you are ready to enter the workforce it is time for you to really execute on this plan in the short term that you (hopefully) have been building on for the past 3-4 years (give or take).

To build out your network, you need to make sure you have one first. As discussed in the previous book, you can use your family contacts or friends and hopefully you have been doing that and maintaining these relationships over the years.

Now, I know this is hard to do. I know that life gets busy and exciting in college and that sometimes the thought of connecting with people makes you shudder. In fact, I have been asked many times as a professor of the Juniors and Seniors if it is ok to reach out to someone they used to know to see if there are any opportunities available. I always give the advice I am giving here in this chapter now. I will go through various scenarios with examples of how to reconnect (or connect). Some of the examples I will provide you with insights on are if:

1. the person is a family friend
2. the person is someone you met and networked with AND kept up with
3. the person is someone you met and networked with and DID NOT keep up with
4. the person is someone who was recommended to you by another person

The general overview and idea of networking is building relationships built on give and take. I discuss the idea of having a circle of networking partners and understanding that you cannot have a very high number of effective networking partners. You need to identify and focus on the people who are more of interest to you and whom you can also help with information and/or other skills and talents. This is the trickiest part. I talk later in this chapter about how we all discount ourselves and what we bring to the table – you do have things or skills or knowledge that is unique and can be used to build effective networking relationships with the right people.

A family friend

If the person is a family friend and you are reaching out to them for the first time or for the hundredth time, you must think about maintaining your professionalism. I mean, if this is someone you called "aunt" or "uncle" growing up, there might be a more relaxed relationship between you. Use your judgement based on the way you have known this person. As with every networking relationship, try to always bring something to the table when you reach out to the person. Do not just email randomly and without giving something in return. Even someone you call "aunt" might get tired of that type of relationship.

With this connection, if it is someone you know personally but have lost touch with, please rely on your shared history in your contact with them so for instance if it is your grammar school basketball coach but you lost touch with her due to time, distance or whatever but you know they work in an industry you are interested in (or they did work in an industry you were interested in), craft an email that reminds of the personal connection and keep it light on the networking aspect (but do try to make a meeting).

For instance, you can email or call with something like this:

"Hi, Jane. I do not know if you remember me but I was on your basketball team in grammar school and I was friends with your child(ren). How are Joe and Jenny? I would love to reconnect with you to see how everything has been with you and your family.

We are all well; I am now in college (yes, sounds crazy, right) and I am studying Accounting and involved in a few activities and an internship, which totally keeps me busy. I am not too busy to connect with you again, though – I will give your office a call next week to see if you have any time to grab a coffee to catch up.

Warmest regards,

Theresa

123-333-4444"

Someone you met and networked with AND kept up with

If the person is someone you met and networked with AND kept up with this is an "easy" continuation in the world of networking. Perhaps the first installment of this book on College Readiness prepared you for the methods and skills of building and maintaining networking relationships. Or maybe you are just a natural networker. These are the ways you will build and grow your career and your skill set by having relationships and partners that guide you and/or that you help guide, too.

Keep up the great work and continue to build and keep these relationships. Know that no one has time to connect with thousands of people on a regular basis – you should have a network of between 30 and 100 people that are relevant and important to your career (and you to theirs).

As much as you can think "Oh, I am just a student I cannot help career professionals." This is the wrong way to think – about just about everything. When I was interviewed via radio show to discuss my book on Entrepreneur-ING, I highlighted extensively about how we all discount ourselves; yes, you are in college and still learning but guess what? Everyone in this world is still learning – if not, they are not living. There is so much to learn and grow on just about daily that you would be surprised how much your new perspective could help a more seasoned career professional or even could help someone just a year or two ahead of you, too.

So keep up the great work on networking and learn more with me in future chapters as we discuss LinkedIn and social media techniques.

Someone you met and networked with and DID NOT keep up with

If the person is someone you met and networked with and DID NOT keep up with do not beat yourself up. Things happen – life gets in the way and no one is perfect. That being said, if you identify who and what is important to you in terms of who you could help and also how you could learn from key people and if these key people did drop out of your circle, do what you can to get them back into your circle of networking. Do not overextend yourself. As I have said already, it is not possible to network with thousands of people effectively. You are looking to build relationships and to maintain them as best you can. Some relationships will change and falter but for the key people in your circle, you want to be able to maintain and continue those relationships.

When you reach out to someone you did not keep in touch with, be conciliatory and respectful. Understand if you do not hear back that the person has moved on and is no longer interested. Do not keep pushing – just try to mend the fact that you ghosted. However, maybe the other person was so busy that they did not notice you ghosted so instead of being over the top apologetic try something like,

"Hi,

I noticed we had not been in touch for some time after meeting at Y. I was thinking about what we last spoke about in terms of XYZ and thought I could add to it now that I have a fresher perspective with this new class I am taking – are you still working on XYZ? What is your new challenge? I would love to catch up and see if there is anything I can help you with in the near future. Let me know how things have been and if you have time to catch up! Yours, Lisa"

This might lead to a rekindled relationship and you can follow up one time after this before you, like Frozen, "Let it go".

Someone who is recommended to you by another person

If the person is someone who was recommended to you by another person, it is important that you follow up with the person and make reference to who suggested that you connect. It can be something worthwhile for both of you but even if not, it shows respect to the initial recommender that you follow through on this connection.

If it is someone on LinkedIn, we will discuss that in Chapter 5. Yes, I could include it here but I think that LinkedIn is so powerful and important to your career that it needs a whole chapter highlighting it and other methods of social media.

Old School Networking

In 2000, I found myself out of work after spending 6 months at Merrill Lynch (at the time known as "Mother Merrill" because people did not leave; in fact one of my co-workers was in his 90's and had spent his whole career with the company) and 6 months at a dot-com (hello late 1990's and the dot com explosion). I was young (only about 23) and needed to figure out how to build a career.

It was a different time and there was a possibility to build a career at one company (which I always knew would not be for me, but I digress).

When I started looking for my next step, I set a deadline by which I wanted to be employed but I did not know how to get results. I was using job boards and submitting my resume everywhere and getting nowhere fast.

While cleaning out my room because I was unemployed and had nothing else to do, I found a handbook I received when I was inducted into an honor society which included a directory of members who had been inducted with their alumni information included and their "current" job information. I went through and identified those who went to St John's University *and* were in the industries I was interested in (mainly financial services at the time). I then created individualized letters for each person and sent them this with my resume:

Dear REDACTED :

Greetings, my name is Lisa A. Vento. I obtained your contact information from the Beta Gamma Sigma Alumni Directory in which you are listed as an alumnus of St. John's University. I am a member of Beta Gamma Sigma and a double alumna of St. John's University.

In light of our shared history with both St. John's University and Beta Gamma Sigma, I was interested in taking the time to send you a personal letter to inform you of my current professional situation. As a business contact that is also a "friend" to St. John's University, I would like to request your assistance in formulating the next step in my career.

I received my BS degree in Marketing, summa cum laude, from the Staten Island Campus in May of 1998. At graduation, during which I was valedictorian, I was awarded a full tuition scholarship and graduate assistantship to the Rome, Italy campus of St. John's University.

As you may know, the MBA program in Rome is a highly intensive one and I graduated with my MBA in International Finance in July 1999 with a 3.96 GPA. Upon my return to the United States, I accepted a position with Merrill Lynch & Co. in the Corporate Policies & Procedures Department.

At Merrill Lynch, I was responsible for both the readability and the accuracy of all internal publications. The Senior Editor aspects of the position morphed into a position with a Total Quality Management focus under my direction. It was a wonderful experience. During my time at Merrill Lynch, an Internet company from the Boston area solicited me to join their small staff. The allure of the position at TimeTo was the value proposition as it appealed to my Vincentian-based education received from St. John's University. TimeTo was interested in bringing families together through the Web. The Internet fallout led to a massive restructuring and a lay off which affected my entire department.

The severance package provided by TimeTo, although not enough to allow for an early retirement, was sufficient to allow me to step back and give thought to my career path. I would like you to assist me in this thought process.

I would like the opportunity to meet with you, at your convenience. Although there might not currently be employment opportunities at your company, I do believe that the more contacts I can meet with to discuss my goals and aspirations, the better formulated my next career step will be. I will contact you early next week to schedule an appointment.

Enclosed, please find my resume, which further details my background and experience.
Thank you.

Sincerely,

Lisa A. Vento

Of 60+ letters I sent out, I met with over 50 people and wound up with a job offer from one of these networking partners. It was a wonderful experience and did lead to some partners that I still am in touch with today over 16 years later. However, this is not how "easy" as it is to build this success route in terms of networking. And by "easy" I can tell you that although it is just a letter you see here, I actually built a database behind this with records for each partner and did some mail merges to help with the customization of the letters and since no one else was doing this, I worried it would be considered an invasion of privacy.

Each person who responded to my letter was humbled and happy to meet with me AND to share my resume with all of their contacts, headhunters etc. Try this now and you will see these types of letters (or more commonly emails) wind up in the trash pile. We just do not have the time to respond to something that is now overdone to death. The point of the social media chapter of this book is to redesign this approach for today.

Chapter 3:

How to Write the Perfect Resume

This can be a whole book. For the past 15+ years, I have been editing and improving and creating resumes for clients, friends, family and students. I discuss in my college and career readiness seminars what inspired me to begin helping people with their resumes. I was lucky enough that during my MBA program (right after my undergrad degree), my resume looked like this:

LISA A. VENTO

Via Santa Maria Mediatrice 24

Roma, Italia 00165

E-mail: lvent010@stjohns.edu

Cellular: 011-39-339-2303055

EDUCATION

Masters of Business Administration in International Finance,   July 1999 3.98/4.0

 St. John's University   Rome, Italy

 Bachelor of Science in Marketing 1998, 3.9/4.0

 St. John's University New York, USA

EXPERIENCE

September 1998- St. John's University Rome, Italy

Present   Graduate Assistant to the Director

- Responsible for the Admissions procedure of the University
- Maintain a database of all international applicants
- Coordination of special events including Graduations
- Collect and analyze statistical information regarding students and faculty
- Contact person for all University inquiries in both Italian and English
- Coordinate all scheduling for administrative staff

June 1997-   St. John's University   New York, USA

May 1998   Information Technology Assistant

- Assistant in the use of teleconferencing equipment for high level meetings
- Upgraded memory and installed 16x CD-ROM drive in IBM computers

July 1994-

May 1997   Admissions Office

- Promoted membership to the High School Relations Society
- Conducted information tours of the campus

May 1996-   Macfadden Trade Publishing   New York, NY

August 1996 Marketing Assistant Internship

- Assistant in the use of teleconferencing equipment for high level meetings
- Upgraded memory and installed 16x CD-ROM drive in IBM computers
- Conducted marketing research to executives in the retail convenience store industry
- Assisted in the coordination of the "Top 50 Forum" in Chicago an annual trade show/gala used to recognize the top convenience stores in the industry
- Designed competitive analysis reports for publication industry

SKILLS   Windows NT, 95 and 3.11, Microsoft Office, WordPerfect, Internet

LANGUAGES   English, Italian

HONORS

Awarded a full graduate scholarship and assistantship to the Rome campus of St. John's University

Class Valedictorian

New York State Champion - Debating Society 1998

Northeast Regional Champion - Debating Society 1998

Recipient of 20 trophies at National Speech and Debate Competitions

Significant Student Award 1994-1995, 1996-1997

St. John's University Woman of Achievement Award
1996-1997, 1997-1998

MEMBERSHIPS

The President's Society (the highest honor that can be bestowed on an undergraduate)

Dean's List 1995, 1996, 1997, 1998

Golden Key National Honor Society 1997-1998

Beta Gamma Sigma, AACSB International Honor Society

Omicron Delta Epsilon, International Honor Society in Economics

Historian, Phi Beta Lambda (National Business Honor Society)

That is an old school resume and it was found via my old Monster account as I do not have it saved as an original Word document anymore. I still think this is one of my best resumes and when I show it to the students I teach, they are always kind of impressed / hate me / want to steal it. I had the balance of experience (internships and GA roles) and honors, activities, memberships and more. This resume got me into amazing interviews even up against Ivy League students – I was able to hold my own even coming from a more "humble" university and being from Staten Island.

That being said, once I returned to the United States and began my career is when I took some missteps. As someone with an MBA and limited work experience, I was too qualified for some jobs and underqualified for the bulk of other jobs. My first position was my immediate hope to get paid for something – and it was maybe not the perfect fit or career position that I should have been looking for and I think this is all relevant even today for those of you who want to graduate with a job offer.

You want to have that job offer but you also should want it to be on a career path for your future. I am a huge proponent of the idea of a "reboot" button and how the idea of knowing what you want to do for your whole career at this point in time as an undergraduate can be impossible.

That being said, in 6 months after graduation, you start getting your student loan bills and of course you want to have a position and be bringing in salary as opposed to continuing to work in retail and/or to be looking for a real job. I think in this economy in 2016 and beyond, you need to keep moving. And having a job offer and beginning the process of having a 401(k) or 403(b) is more important that focusing on career planning, per se.

You should still keep an eye on your ultimate career plan and you should use my Entrepreneur-ING book 1 to identify your plans and keep those in focus. I really feel that is the perfect next book for you to read in a year or two once you actually start your path in having experience. Remember, the old issue with needing experience to get a job and needing a job to get experience is still something that exists.

For me, I had a resume review done by someone recommended by a networking partner. I went into that meeting thinking my resume was golden and left with more red marks on my resume than I ever thought possible. It opened my eyes to the art and nuance of resume reviews and it also shocked me because the person who "reviewed" my resume ripped it and me apart so it showed me that there was a need for resume review with compassion – so constructive criticism instead of scorched earth.

That being said, how to write the best resume for you is based off of the simple principles from my resume in 1999 that matched your age and experience potential. Let's walk through the sections that you should have to blow your competition out of the water.

Header & Footer

I start my lesson with the header and the footer. Why? Because these are the pieces that catch the eye first – particularly the header. What I like to do here for my clients is to set the header with the name of the person in larger font (like 15 point) and I never put home addresses. I think these documents wind up all over so I do not leave the address field. I include a QR code built around LinkedIn profile. (More on LinkedIn profile in Chapter 5.)

The QR code can be made, for free, via various websites, such as

www.qr-code-generator.com/ or you can do a Google search for "free QR Code Generator". Once in the site, you can put in the LinkedIn address or if you have a blog or any other online portfolio, you can use that link to create the QR code. You save it as a JPEG and make it smaller to place on the header. See my Website for more information on this at www.thenextstep1234.com/blog QR Codes.

If you have a specific focus you want to highlight such as accounting or marketing, you can include it in your name field. For example,

Jane Smith, Marketing Major

Or

Joe Jones, Accounting Major dual program

Under the name field, you put your cell and email address. Note on email addresses must be repeated – have a normal email address such as firstname.lastname@gmail.com. If you cannot find your name, use first initial and last name or some other combination. Your school email is an ok idea but once you graduate you may or may not continue access to that email – every school handles dormant or former student emails differently so if your resume outlives your email address, that would not be good. Your cell phone should be a normal outgoing message, although since so few of this generation uses their cell phones for "talking", I would imagine this would not be an issue except your outgoing message might be the default message of the number of your phone. This should be changed to be something like,

"Hello, you have reached Joe Jones. I cannot come to the phone right now but if you leave a detailed message with your call back number, I will get back to you as soon as I can. Thanks!"

Or something to that affect. These are basic information that you all might know about but I would be doing a disservice if I did not include the basics because it helps everyone start from the same base.

The footer is a different story and dependent on your background and work experience. A rule of thumb about resumes is that new college graduates should only have one page, meaning the footer can just be your name.

However, for some of you who have read and followed my advice from the first installment in this series, The Book on College Readiness, you might find you have more content to include and share on your resume. I am going to say if you are on point with lots of internships (at least 2) and activities (at least 2-4), your resume can be two pages. I would not suggest going over 2 pages, though. That would be excessive.

If the resume is two pages, the footer should include your name and page number, as you like it to look.

This high level information is just that and should not be too large of spaces for header or footer. If you put the QR code you can shrink it so it just takes up a small corner on the page and if you are really good, you can set it so that it only shows on the first page header. (Option in Word for different first page header).

Objective/Summary

This can be tough; some objectives can be trite or just weird. It can be hard to sum up who you are and what you are looking for in your career search in one sentence. I tend to leave the Objective out *except* for specific job applications and then I want it to be original each time. Such as, "Objective: To begin my career with KPMG as an accountant."

So tailored to the job at hand. You do have to make cover letters (more on that in Chapter 4) and they can be done via email or other messaging service.

The Summary is something I create for all of my clients and it is different each time. I assume that everyone reading resumes has limited time – in fact, most resumes are looked at for a total of 3-5 seconds in the first round of reviews. If you survive that review, then you will get a bit longer look before you are even considered to be brought in for an interview.

I like to see right under the Objective (if one is used) a collection of bullet points highlighting the important stuff in your background such as languages you speak, specializations of skills, interesting internships and more. If you do not have anything to put here, think again. You can include your degree and information on any skills or talents that can be brought up and highlighted. This should not be just copied and pasted but written from scratch to highlight the most important things about you while also being included in the body of the resume. This is for the quick glance to make sure you do not get overlooked because your language skills were buried at end of page 1 or even page 2.

Education

This is the last time that Education will be highlighted up top for most resumes. If you want a job in Academia then education will always be on top because you will be in school forever until you get a PhD (ba dum dum).

The school should be listed first with the city and state such as:

ABC University   **City, State**

Under that should be your field of study and graduation date – if the date has not come yet, you must label is "Anticipated" such as:

BS in Marketing   May 2016, anticipated

 You can and should include your GPA if it is over a 3.0; if your overall GPA is over a 3.0, include it. If the overall GPA is not over 3.0 but your major GPA is you can include that GPA but label it appropriately. If you have any notable scholarships based off of your high school and/or college performance based achievement, it can be included here.

Activities and Leadership

This section can be next if you have stuff to include. If you do not have Activities and Leadership, skip right to the Experience section next.*

*Author's Note: This is where you can include your activities; if you feel your experience is more applicable and important, you can put that section before this one.

I know recruiters, hiring managers and more like to see the "well rounded" student. Meaning that they have the GPA and the experience and the activities, too. GPA is important but it is not as important as the full criteria set of GPA, experience and activities. More and more what is being valued is the unique-ness the ability to create something and to show you can balance. Balance was always important, though even for me over 20 years ago the fact that I had activities, internships and experience was the key to many job interviews and offers.

In this economy and in this market, the college degree is not as important or esteemed as it once was for previous generations. It used to be a huge deal to have a Bachelor's degree but now it is almost the level of a high school diploma in terms of "prestige" and what you are worth to the job market. I do hope you had already read my The Book on College Readiness to have known that going significantly into debt to have a degree from a certain school is not really the right way to be ahead of the game.

Having activities, leadership and experience can help you position yourself to graduate with a job offer even if your GPA is not as high as you would like it to be for the resume.

If you have enough time before graduation and realize this section of your resume is a little light, please consider what you can get involved in at your school. Depending on your major, there have to be groups and societies that exist about it or if you have interests in co-curricular type of activities see if you can get involved now. You can include these on your resume but do not be disingenuous. Do not pretend to have done it for all 4 years though you can leave date information off of all of your activities and leadership to help build this out. If you are asked about it specifically during an interview, you can talk about how you found it later in your college career and how much you learned/gave back/experienced while doing it.

Experience

If you read the first book in this series, this should be a done deal for you. Having experience in the forms of internships, externships and/or paid work is so important to your resume and your next step. I hope you have some great company names to put here, some great activities and some great references, to boot.

Whatever you did at your various experiences, be honest but also be artful in your wording. If you opened and sorted the mail, you can say that but it might be better to say, "Researched, analyzed and shared daily reports for the staff." Do not stretch the truth so much as explain what you do in terms of project / process management and/or management level tasks.

Every year that I teach, I ask my students if they want to be a manager and across the board, they never do. Because being a manager means you are responsible for others, their work, their careers and more. However, today and over the last several years I have had to explain that everyone who works anywhere IS a manager. You are responsible for other's deliverables and timelines no matter what even if you are the newest hire. Everything is project and team based and if you can convey and show that you are a great team player AND a great motivator by your experiences (or your activities and leadership roles, for that matter) you will be the top choice for any company.

Skills

If you learned a lot of computer and technical skills, I would argue for having a "Soft Skills" and a "Tech Skills" section. If you have just basic computer skills, you can leave this in one section. Please do not forget to list all of your skills. Please do not list "great communicator" in this section. You can tell that skillset better in your experience and activities and leadership sections then you ever could by referencing it here.

Language

If you know any other language in any capacity include it here and just in case you do not know this by now, always be honest. If you put you are fluent in French, do not be surprised if the company wants to conduct your interview in French. I will say though that for many people whom I help with their resumes, they forget to include languages. It is important to include it and to be clear on fluency levels. You can use "native language", "near-fluency", "fluent", "conversational", or "basic".

References

This can just be listed though some people would say it is not needed. It can just be References – Available upon request or you can include your references, in the event that it is a job you really would like or the company asks for this information. Please try to inform the people you select as references that you will be putting their information – frame it as a question. For instance,

"Mr Mcdonald, would it be all right if I included you as a reference for my future opportunities?"

You can ask this over email, phone or message depending on your relationship. It is acceptable to have a teacher be a reference but you should have at least 1-2 "managers" in the sense of work world and a few professors. Even better is a professor who helped "moderate" one of your groups or activities that you either took part in or led.

Overall, the resume should be crisp and focused on showcasing what is the best of you. It should provide insight into how great you are at multi-tasking and learning. Learning is key and if you have taken any extra skill-based trainings or thought about how you want to apply your degree to real world work, this must be included and shown in your resume.

This could be shown via your work experience, if any or your train of studying. Maybe you took extra seminars or training offered via your job(s) or your university? Maybe you provided training at a local school in a partnership relationship between your university and your community. This would be really key – to showcase your ability to both teach and learn at the same time, can show you to be a great candidate for any job.

A note on paper- many resumes are now sent and shared electronically and I feel it is less of a big deal to submit a paper copy. Also, your LinkedIn profile (to be covered in Chapter 5) is the real key to your job search and potential in terms of introducing companies to you and your background. For contacts that ask for a hard copy of your resume, I do think it is still important to use a resume paper but it should be cream or white for entry level positions and searches. The envelope should match and when you send follow up thank you notes and correspondence, you should use the resume paper unless you want to make a statement with sending regular paper. I am not too interested in the paper type you use – so long as it is crisp and looks great printed.

A note on font – people are continually talking about how Times New Roman is "dead" but I am not convinced. Many people in the hiring roles are straining their eyes to read resumes with small font to squeeze on one page as it is and at least we know Times New Roman is readable. You can expand to Helvetia or Arial Narrow, if you wish. Watch the font size, though as your resume must be readable. If you need 2 pages, go for it. Keep the font at least as a size 9 through 11. You definitely do not need 12 or larger because that will just look like you are trying too hard to fill space.

Also, tweaking your resume (as needed) for specific job searches is a good thing to do. Having the right key words in your resume or LinkedIn profile or your job application can lead to more results. Carefully review the job listing and see what you should add and/or highlight in your resume.

As you begin your career, there is more to think about in terms of being focused and ready for your next step and for that, I will recommend again The Prof's Guide to Entrepreneur-ING Using Entrepreneurial Skills to Launch Your Own Business or be the Boss of Your Career.

Chapter 4

How to Write Your Cover Letter to Get Noticed

The cover letter can be a disaster and can get you infamy, ignored or interviewed.

First on infamy. There have been many cases in the past (particularly with social media) where cover letters have become mocked and shared virally on how badly they were written and/or showcased the person's "bragging" or "boasting" to the nth degree. This has happened particularly in financial services where people mistake the industry culture as one they see in the movies and move ahead with letters written beyond the shade of insanity.

You want to avoid any form of "infamy" in your job search. You want to make sure you are not being unnecessarily boastful, ridiculous or otherwise rude.

The second category of cover letters are the "ignored" ones – this is due to spelling or grammatical mistakes or otherwise poorly written letters that betray you as being not focused and/or looking like a bad candidate.

You have to remember that hiring manager and/or whoever is receiving and reviewing these applications on the first round is honed to look for these red flags in applications. If your cover letter for instance spells the company's name wrong or has other elementary issues with spelling or grammar, yours will be thrown out without a second glance.

Interviewed is the category you want to fall into – the best way to do this is to highlight your skills and talents as they apply to the company and/or the job you are interested in getting an interview. The letter has to be well written and if you follow my tips in this chapter, you will fall into this category more often than not.

Types of Cover Letters

There are different ways of using cover letters and for my purposes of lessons in this chapter, I am breaking them up as:

- online job submission
- personal contact
- job inquiry cover letter
- response to a listing (actual job board)
- email cover letter (which will include a real cover letter attached to it, anyway)

Some quick points to keep in mind – all letters should follow a business format. Use the header you have on your resume as the header of your cover letter. You can include your mailing address here, although I leave it off on the resume.

The idea is to have your name and email and cell phone number information in the header.

Then go down the left side of the document and type in just your address (you do not need your name there again) and then hit enter a few times, put the date. The date should be of the day when you print it. Then put in the addressee name and mailing address.

At this point you hit enter a few times again and type either To Whom it May Concern (only if you do not know who it is for) or Dear Mr/Mrs XYZ. If it is a close friend, you can use first name only BUT I would err on the side of being professional and addressing professionally.

You then press enter again and begin typing in paragraph forms your information. Always begin with a greeting or salutation of some sort. Then state clearly what you are contacting them for or who asked you to contact them. So if it is just for a job that you do not know the person you would just state, "I am applying for the BLANK position at your company." Then you have to write WHY you should get an interview – I would say write why you should get the job but this is much harder to do. We just would like to at least get in the door for an interview so you can wow them with the other lessons and skills I am going to teach you in this book on how to interview. Demonstrate (with key points that are also on your resume) why you would be a great candidate to interview for this position. Make this section a paragraph or two.

Do NOT write a 2-4 page letter; all cover letters should be short, sweet and super powerful at demonstrating why the hiring manager or person should turn the page and review the resume and maybe call you in. It goes without saying to make sure there are NO spelling errors and NO grammatical errors. Also, you must type full sentences in all communication methods – even email. Do not shorten anything in "text" speak.

A rough draft of what your template should look like is below.

Header – Name

Anything important (licensing, etc.)

Cell   Professional email

Your Street Address

City, State Zip Code

DATE

FULL ADDRESS TO WHOM IT IS GOING

To whom it may concern (OR NAME),

Greetings, my name is XX and I am applying for the XYZ job (or I was asked to send this letter from XYZ...)

DEMONSTRATIVE PARAGRAPHS (2 of them) from your resume as to why you should be interviewed for the role. Use real examples from your resume to build this out as best you can.

Any language skills or extraordinary skills should be included, as well.

Closing paragraph should be something that implies how to connect to set up an appointment.

Sincerely,

Your Name

Online Job Submission

I am starting with online job submission because so much of our job searches are done using the online world of job applications.

Many jobs are listed online at job boards, company websites or other search functionality. I recommend Indeed.com – there is an app and everything that you can tailor the job search to send you results every day via email and/or use the app to review jobs in your interest area/location area and you can submit the resume often times via the app itself (but sometimes you do need to go further and submit via computer using the company website functions).

For these, sometimes, there is a text box asking you to add in your cover letter either via copy and paste or typing free hand OR giving you the option to upload the Word file. If you must type it free hand, please copy and paste into Word before you hit submit as we are all horribly dependent on using a spell check before we submit anything to anyone.

If you can, I would prefer that you have a Word template for a cover letter on your computer and that you personalize it each time for the jobs you want to apply to using this online submission. I know, I know that this is annoying and time consuming but if you want results that count, this extra step is worth it. If you are just looking and you have a year or two before graduation then by all means, use one cover letter and do not personalize it to the job at hand BUT most of these apps will not be looked at because the instructions often say to include the job in the cover letter.

Have the base letter on your desktop and tweak it as necessary. Make sure it hits on the right skills and talents as much as you can – so review the job listing and include as much as you can that you actually have in your resume and your abilities. Do not exaggerate here – if it asks for fluency in Russian or database programming do NOT say you are fluent in these things unless you truly are.

Having the right keywords in the cover letter (or resume) that match to the job listing gives you a better shot of getting to the next step. Again, it goes without saying to have the letter fall into the "interview" category and not the infamy or ignored one. The best way to do this is to read the letter out loud and to share it with some friends, family and/or trusted professional (like me). Do this more with the base letter to make sure it is as perfect as possible but then remember to review the additions appropriately to make sure it does not ruin the letter.

Personal Contact

Here is when you can use an actual letter (or see email cover letter below). You can reach out to your network and/or friends and family with a mailed cover letter and resume. For this, use resume paper and an envelope that is printed using a computer or with a printed label on it.

You should have the letter read professionally and indicate clear next steps in the letter. For instance, if you would like to meet in person to discuss your background then put that in the letter. If you would just like to share your background via resume with this contact so that they can present your resume around their company, explain that in the letter.

Always establish a feedback loop, though. So even if the person asked you to send you the resume and cover letter, always include in the letter that you will follow up at some point in the future to find out if there is anything else you can do. If this is a close networking person or relative or friend, you can ask them to tell you any feedback on the resume they might have. You can word this in such a way that you can ask it of anyone who you are sending this exploratory resume and cover letter to via mail.

If you choose to send this via email, see the section via email cover letters below.

Job Inquiry Cover Letter

Perhaps someone recommended you submit your application to a job in real life. You need to send a cover letter and resume through the mail and this should be as close to perfect as possible. If you know the job description and other information then you can personalize the letter or email specifically to the person and always highlight who recommended you. Do not feel that you cannot include that information – it is quite important to pull together that connection to the forefront of the letter you send so that your paperwork gets the appropriate attention.

Hopefully the networking partner that recommended you is in good standing and your papers will be put on top of the list. If the person who recommended you is not the "right" person, know that this might not help you but it also might not hurt you necessarily. It can go either way. It is always better to know someone than not to.

Response to a Listing (actual job board)

These are literally like looking for a needle in a haystack in terms of getting responses from these submissions. You must be on point – there are tons of other people filling out applications for these roles, too. If it says to include a cover letter and you do not, your information will not be reviewed.

If there are ten or more pages or "screens" to fill out and you do not do them all, you cannot submit the application. Filling these things out can be a job in itself. It is rarely a simple process. Some job sites are more simplistic than others and allow for a simple loading of a resume file. However, no matter what, your resume must be perfect. If you load it and the system reformats it, you have to go in and manually edit it to make it looks "attractive".

Depending on what field you want to go into, there are tons of specific job boards and company websites that also accept applications and resumes. My advice is to use Indeed.com because you can set up detailed job searches and that service will look through multiple job sites and company information to pull the best matches. Have a few different searches set up to your email and some you can apply from your phone (there is an app with this site, too which makes this more "seamless".)

That being said, while it is possible to find a job this way but the other ways are more powerful and more based on human relations and networking and therefore more results can arise from the other options.

This does not mean you should give up on job sites. You should continue to apply for positions that appeal to you BUT do not make this your only path to employment. You must use the other options discussed in this chapter and in future chapters to best be ready to graduate with a job offer.

Email cover letter

All of the above advice on cover letters applies to the email cover letter, too. My advice is to include an attachment to this email that includes an "official" cover letter. The email should not match exactly the cover letter; you can keep it short and sweet and really focus on your subject line because people are inundated with emails on a daily basis and it is easy to get "lost" in the inbox.

Your subject line should tie in to how you found the person – were you recommended to contact them by someone? If so, put that in the subject line, "Joe Louis recommended that I email you about X".

If you are applying for a job and this poor person's email was put on the instructions to submit resume and cover letter materials, put in the subject line your name and exactly what position you are applying for so that the person can see right away how to categorize your response.

If you are "cold" emailing the person and have no connection but have researched them, make your subject line as intriguing as possible without sounding crazy OR spammy. You want to stand out to get opened but this is one of the hardest ways to make a connection used alone. You would also have to follow up via phone calls and make yourself a resource to the person to make them interested in meeting with you and/or even responding to you at all.

The email then should include a nice greeting and a quick paragraph about why you are contacting them and referencing the attached cover letter.

Such as,

"Dear Jane,

[How you know them – either recommended to contact them or the job listing said to email them or you are cold emailing them.]

[Then a couple of sentences detailing why they should open your attachments (resume and cover letter). This should be appealing and quick and enticing to get them to actually open your attachments.]

Warmest regards,

Your Name

Note: No matter how you connect with the people or why, your cover letter and resume should be as close to perfect as possible and your tone and writing style should be engaging and interesting to get them interested in following up with you.

Chapter 5:

Using LinkedIn and Other Social Media to Stand Out for the Right Reasons

This is my sweet spot of advice and focus as someone who travels around and gives speeches at various youth orientated events to teach how to use social media (including LinkedIn) to build your BRAND. I know this sounds crazy – a "brand" you are thinking to yourself, "I am not a 'brand' I am a person! I'm not Coca-Cola!" Well, it is time for you to think of yourself as Coca-Cola or something like it – it is important for you to begin using social media strategically to get yourself noticed in the right way.

There is a way to balance this to also embrace your "youth" but I will say that I am thankful every day that social media did not exist in my youth as it does now. End of story. I would have had to move and get plastic surgery and change my name if I had been able to "broadcast" the way today's youth can. I tell this story a lot as a professor but when I was in high school and college, if I got into an argument with my boyfriend or got dumped or something, the only ones who would know about it were my close friends if and when I saw them, passed them a note in the hallway or called them on the landline after school.

Today, when something like this happens, everyone knows because it gets broadcast on social media to your nearest and dearest what, 500+ friends (Facebook) or the WHOLE internet (Twitter).

I caution against using Facebook and other social media as an online diary. You should have a more "professional" looking social media by perhaps having two accounts one for "public" and the other for "private". However, I caution against this too because it gives a false sense of security that is not really possible. As I talk about my The Book on College Readiness, you are paying colleges to accept you so barring anything really inflammatory or viral, you will be accepted to a point. Of course, if your profile is embarrassing or otherwise makes your look like a poor student, you might lose out on scholarships or something else.

For careers, though, the way to lose out on a job interview or job offer is much higher – if your social media looks unprofessional or otherwise ethically challenged or just downright politically incorrect, you might never know why but you will not get invited for interviews and/or offered a job.

My advice is to do a Google search on both your name and a reverse image search of one of your photos. I would also suggest setting up a Google alert for your name to make sure you know what is out there about you at all times.

I caution my seminar and workshop attendees to not post photos in the state of undress and I am just going to go down in the books as a total prude by saying to judiciously post bikini or bathing suit pictures. Also, no duck face photos, please or at least not too many of them. For the guys, no photos of you inside with sunglasses which I am hearing is the equivalent of duck face.

Keep your content you share on any social media service "clean" – no racy jokes, no over-involvement in politics - offices do NOT want to hire a zealot of any kind whether that be someone obsessed with a particular political party or religion or celebrity. Once you are hired, a company is "stuck" with you and will not tolerate dealing with someone who is too extreme.

No matter what, when you first start out you have to be considered "malleable" and not "risky" – you have no "real" work experience to stand on to show you are a great employee (even if you have tons of internships and part time work, this is not weighed the same as having spent 1-5 years in an office somewhere) – you are a risk for any firm and if you are doing things on social media that make you stand out in a "negative" way, you are proving you are not worth the risk.

Take away the "risk" and keep your social media as professional as possible. Depending on your age, you can still be "youthful" but remember "youthful" is not code word for "excuse". Do not let anything be posted that can be used to denigrate your personality, your professionalism or your potential.

For your personality, avoid looking mercurial or nasty online. There are joke-y type things you might want to post but really think three times before you hit "tweet" or "enter" because what you might think of as funny could be considered nasty at best or downright nuclear level of insanity at worst. What is downright nuclear level of insanity? Think of the many examples of people who tweet something and then go viral (for bad reasons) and then wind up fired and/or otherwise vilified in the press.

For your professionalism, consider thinking in terms of a young professional. You can still use social media in a youthful way but without following the crowd too much. Beware of "FOMO" the fear of missing out – just because everyone else is posting bikini or bathing suit pictures or talking bad about their teachers online does not mean you have to do the same.

Beware the sense of false security that comes with "oh, this is set to private". No matter how "private" you might be set up as, someone can still snap a picture of it and share it somewhere else and no matter what, once something is on the internet, just assume it is there forever.

Try to sprinkle in some professional postings – or sharing articles or photos of things you are interested in or have accomplished. Consider using social media to build your brand and your portfolio to have stuff to share that might make you stand out for the right reasons.

This is how you show and build your potential. Showing another side of yourself in terms of a passion project or work you have done or even just sharing stuff about an industry or about cooking or something you like is a good way to provide a better rounded snapshot of who you are and what you can do.

Rough Plan for all Social Media & Building Your Online "Portfolio"

Share things that reflect you in terms of the whole you.

Shy away from sharing things that are too personal. Hint: If you are crying and/or hysterical laughing, maybe step away from the internet and do not share it.

Use what I call the "breadcrumb method" to sprinkle in bits and pieces of your professionalism or something you are interested in or something to do with the industry you want to work in through your social media posts. I am not advocating that you become insufferable on social media but try to include pieces of what makes you interested in jobs, careers and/or just your own passions. For instance, if you are a great cook, you can include that in your social media with the posts about your favorite TV show or celebrity.

Be thoughtful in your posts – try not to post things without thinking. It is so easy to get into this world where we "document" our lives for the world to see and we try to present ourselves in a certain light – when young, you want to be seen as fun, happening, at the right places, etc. I think this is ok to continue but you should be using that breadcrumb method to also be including what makes you special, unique and hirable!

You can include your portfolio pieces here – include a link to your most recent paper or group project, see if a Professor will let you video tape one of your presentations for use on social media to promote both your work and your class. You would be surprised but some professors might be able to let you do this (depending on the rules of the university, of course).

If you cannot video it in class, do a practice run and grab that on video and then you can post it as you wish.

You can compile and create your own "online portfolio" that can be used as you deem fit. You can create, for free, a website with service provides such as Weebly.com. You could create a website with simple design and just a few clicks – I am sure there are tons of other providers but I know Weebly best. You create it for free with your name as the URL so firstnamelastname.weebly.com would be the URL that you get for free. You can then build it out and create links to papers, presentations and even videos.

This can become a big part of your social media focus OR you can just create it and drive people to it via your resume, applications etc where you can use the QR code function to scan to it or just include it as a direct link on your resume for people to find out more about your skills, writing talents, presentation abilities, communication abilities and more.

LinkedIn

This is the absolute thing to do for your social media and your future. If you are dead set against posting "professional" things in your other social media accounts because maybe you only use a spoof account where you post obsessively about Keeping Up with the Kardashians or something (please let it be in a fake name and not trackable to you...) Ok, so let's say you just are not comfortable using Instagram and/or Twitter or Facebook to promote who you are as a professional (soon to be) – that is ok – I mean, I do not agree with it but I can understand it.

As someone who has worked with youth for the past 13+ years, I know that reputations can die or thrive based off of the "coolness" factor of your social media. Even typing that I showed how "old" and out of touch I am – and I get it – and I think you get the sentiment. That social media is a way to be the cool kid in school and beyond by showing this cultivated life of fun and craziness more so than papers and interviewing techniques.

So, this is where "LinkedIn" comes in – the stodgy form of social media, I guess. This is where you can build out your professional personality and you can start by compiling your portfolio here. You can use the Weebly website reference above to share content with LinkedIn – you can just link the content from Weebly to LinkedIn. Conversely, if the idea of building your own website makes you panic, you can just create your portfolio here in LinkedIn by posting and sharing your presentations, papers and more.

LinkedIn is an overlooked tool but it is where the most opportunity is for anyone – employee, new graduate, entrepreneur, etc. For me, once I began using LinkedIn appropriately, I unlocked tons of opportunity for my business and sometimes I do wish I had known and used it better when I was career focused in corporate America so by default then, I have the best advice and lessons for YOU to use this tool to get the edge on building your career.

A few years ago, one of my connections began sharing news articles and doing other interactive posts on LinkedIn and I remember thinking he/she was annoying and crazy. I was the one who was annoying and crazy. By using LinkedIn in this small way, they were sharing their name and expertise across the platform and getting noticed by hiring managers, headhunters and more.

When you use LinkedIn appropriately, you can build out a professional and expert level background quickly and "safely". You do have to be careful how you use the service; you do not want to spam it nor share things that do not belong on a professional site.

That being said, as I instruct my professional clients with 10+ years' experience the same can be done for you "newbies", you start small. Begin my joining relevant groups in your industry and engaging in posts, providing your opinion or creating posts of your own about questions or ideas around that subset industry page.

Then you can use your profile page to post "updates" such as a recent paper you wrote that you would like to share for professional input or asking for people to interview for a campus project (almost everyone loves to talk about themselves and get "free" press). If you make the process simple enough like, "I will call you and interview you, at your convenience", you would be surprised how much response you can get AND how many personal relationships you can make this way.

This is the meat of it - your LinkedIn contacts might be people you know in real life or people you want to know in real life and by including an interactive response you can try to build on these relationships outside of the internet realm. These relationships grounded in real conversations and events are more actionable and more meaningful than just saying "I have 100-500 LinkedIn connections."

Use LinkedIn as a tool to build real relationships. When you meet someone at a networking event, find them on LinkedIn and connect with them or ask them to connect with you referencing your recent in person meeting. Then continue to interact with these individuals either in posting informative news and updates and/or reaching out with an occasional message through the system or even better to their own email account and sharing something that would help them. Keep in mind this is not something you have to do daily it is not something you have to do weekly – just every couple of months, if something makes you think of one of your networking partners or what they are working on or doing, share it with them.

Also consider creating content using the LinkedIn Pulse functionality. Maybe you wrote a paper that can be added to and/or edited to fit into a "news" item – do it. Share it on LinkedIn Pulse and it goes beyond your network and brings your name to other people who maybe did not think of you before.

Include your volunteer activities and other personal details, as it fits. For instance, if you work with abused animals and have a passion for helping animals, if you include that in your profile then that could help you build connections with like-minded people who would have normally passed on your profile but want to connect for that reason.

This is just the tip of the iceberg on how you can use and benefit from LinkedIn. Make sure your keywords pop, make sure your information in summary and job descriptions shine and ask for and provide references for people so that you can build out that in one place stand-alone guide to all that makes you a great professional to add to any company or team.

Chapter 6:

On Interviewing

There is so many resources and information out there on how to interview but I come at it in a different way. I have written and shared countless advice and input on interviewing both as a professor for 13 years and in my blog for anyone to learn from me and my tips.

Now, having a new platform to document and share this information is beyond amazing. Interviewing is dreaded by most people. Why is it dreaded? It is because it includes the things most of us love to hate the most - public speaking, interacting and make small talk and communicating well.

In my college and career readiness seminars and workshops I spend extra time talking about how to communicate well – or at least how to be a "good" communicator. You do not need to be "great" you do not need to be amazing and giving Ted talks but you do need to have some basic communication skills that can and will give you an edge during interviewing.

You can learn more about these generalized communication skill sets in the first installment of these series, The Book on College Readiness. Hopefully, you have taken part in activities that could help you build out and enhance your communication skills.

If you have not done that yet, it is never too late. You can focus on using your skills in communication in small ways every day. Instead of sitting in class playing on your smartphone while waiting for the professor to arrive and be ready, make some small talk with fellow students. This is a low risk way to build out some conversational skills and if I know anything about the college aged student today vs the student of 13 or even 10 years ago is that the temptation to just play on the phone is so large- I mean, you could be watching a movie, texting someone in another country, who knows what. I get it. It is an amazing device but it is not helping your communication skills.

Try to make small talk with your fellow students, your professors and anyone you come in contact with at internships or networking events. Know how to answer interview questions. Know how to answer almost any question by referencing your resume, telling a story and building a personal connection.

We will talk more in the next few chapters about interviewing one on one vs in groups and using media for interviewing, too. For now, just think about the ways you can appear cool, calm and collected under any circumstance.

I wish I could tell you that the high pressure interview or the bad cop/good cop routine did not exist in interviewing but unfortunately it DOES exist. Sometimes it is done to test you and sometimes people are just jerks. Something to always remember is to use your gut to try to identify and decipher the work culture or the work environment. If the place does not feel "right", if people look more miserable than normal on a Monday at 8am or if you just get the sense or vibe that you would not fit in at the place, consider using your options to NOT accept a position or pursue a job in this place.

Many of my students ask me if they should interview somewhere they do not have any interest in working at and my advice is to always go for it because interviewing is a numbers game – it is based off of practice making perfect. There are not many things where this can hold true unequivocally like it does in interviewing. The more interviews you go on, the better you will get at it if you keep an open mind and learn and watch for signs of if you are doing well or not from the interviewer. If you are invited to interview somewhere, you should go and you just do not know – you might think you are uninterested in the company or the position but you could be surprised. Worst case, you spent a couple of hours doing something that was not good for you right now but that did give you exposure to answering more questions and becoming more comfortable in the interview setting.

Always dress professionally for any interview; it is better to be overdressed than underdressed. For women, beware clothing that is too revealing because you just do not realize in advance how much you have to bend during an interview – you have to bend to pick up your bag, to move your stuff around, etc. Make sure you do the test of how revealing an outfit is before the interview day.

For women it is also important to be professional and dress in subdued colors depending on the industry, though. If you are interested in being in a marketing or new start-up environment, you might be able to be more daring in terms of colors and design but for most other industries it is about being professional and put together. You do not have to spend a lot of money on anything except focus on the shoes. Shoes are the first thing noticed; if they are ill-fitting, scuffed and/or inappropriate (such as lucite heels), this could be a deal breaker.

For men, the shoes are one of the most important things. Suits are suits are suits – yes, I know and realize the difference between an off the rack and a $2,000 suit. However for interviewing as a college student, this is not expected to be at the high end of wardrobe. A simple suit in a basic color blue, black or grey is the best way to go. Save the seersucker and/or bright color for other events.

If you feel confident in your clothing and of course neat hair styles – for women, if you have a tendency to play with your hair, wear it up. For men, keep your hair neat and tidy and any facial hair should also be presentable. I would err on the side of clean shaven for most any industry.

The most important "tricks" to interviewing is to be personable, presentable and present. Many people worry and panic before interviews – in fact, the person across the table from you might also be nervous about having to interview you so be yourself, be authentic and be just the best version of yourself you can be. Most hiring decisions are made within the first 90 seconds. Yes, 90 seconds to determine if you fit in because what I mean by this is that first impressions are so important and it really is about if you would fit in at the company and the interviewer can see sitting with you and working with you over the next 6-12 months or longer.

By being presentable with your clothing and hair style and even your bag/backpack, you can get ahead of the competition for the role and please be present. When you sit in the waiting area, do not use your phone. Even if you are researching the company it will make you look less than professional because everyone will be assuming you are using snapchat or something. Sit nicely and read a newspaper and/or professional magazine. Make small talk with those sitting around you and/or the secretary.

Arrive to the interview location about 30 minutes before your scheduled time but do not go into the building until 15 minutes before. You do not want to be too early or be running late, either. When you arrive, find out how you can enter the building. Always have ID with you as oftentimes you need to show your identification before you can enter a building.

When you arrive, you can scope out where the restrooms are and if you need a bio break, take one after you check in with the reception desk. Be professional and engaging with the staff – treat the reception desk staff as you would your interviewer. You can be friendly but not too friendly.

Get ready to sit and wait until you are called for your interview by reading and making small talk with the other people in the waiting room. Read on more about how to interview in the next chapter!

Chapter 7:

Interviewing Skills for In-Person Interviews

To build off of some of the tips in Chapter 6, you really need to be personable. Even if you are nervous, even if you are thrown to the wolves so to speak into an interview with 5 or more people asking you questions at once you need to be in complete and utter control of your nerves so that you appear relaxed, at ease but not too relaxed and at ease. It is a balance between looking like you do not care and looking like you would live to puke.

Always keep in mind that sometimes interviews go bad. Sometimes this is because the interviewer is trying to see how you react to pressure and sometimes you just get a bad interviewer. I spend a lot of time in my workshops and training conveying that what happens in an interview room has to be left behind when the interview is over – so if the interview is a total failure, if you freeze up or worse say something you consider "stupid" or if the interviewer is rude and/or mean, just brush yourself off and move on. Learn from the experience, but move on.

It is important to be your authentic best self on interviews. If you are shy and it is painful to speak, work with that. Do the best you can to overcome your shyness so you can hold a conversation but do not try to be someone or something that you are not.

Being authentic means you can just let your natural personality shine through but make that personality be your professional personality. If you do not know what it means to be professional, think about it here?

What makes you professional? List 3 things.

_____

_____

_____

When you sit across from the interviewer, be personable, make eye contact and smile. You can have a portfolio out with copies of your most recent resume. You should ask the interviewer if they would like a copy of your resume and if the resume has been updated, you should reference that so that the interviewer has the most recent resume. This is important because as you reference your stories and/or work experience and/or awards and the interviewer does not see it on the resume, they will ask you "Why isn't this on your resume?" so having the updated copies and offering it can avoid this issue.

Use the portfolio to jot down notes and other important things so you can build the thank you letter (more on that in Chapter 9) and so that you can have fodder for follow up questions. Also by jotting down notes, it allows you to break eye contact and gives you something to do during the interview.

When do you feel the most comfortable in a strange situation? What do you need to do before your interview to be comfortable? How can you prepare?

It is most important to practice, practice, and practice. Keep in mind, you might not like the job or want it per se but that does not mean you should not try to get the job during the interview. As I mentioned earlier, the more practice for answering interview questions you get the better it is for you and it is just as hard for you to know in an interview if the job is good for you as hard as it can be for the company to know if you are the right person for a job.

So always keep an open mind but remember to listen to your gut. Sometimes, you know right away that the company would not work for you. Sometimes, that first impression can be wrong.

Know your resume inside and out and set up stories to tell for the basic interview questions that you know you will always hear.

I am sure if we were in a classroom together you would know the questions.

How about these below and each question should be answered by you but then review how I would suggest you answer them in the paragraphs below. These should be answered with stories from your resume that illustrate how you succeeded, how you did what you said and how you would fit in and hit the ground running at this company for this job.

I will provide you with my thoughts and suggestions for how to answer these questions below. You need to start on your own thoughts on these questions. The more you practice and work on these questions the more prepared you will be for your interviewing. Preparation is the key to having the best interview possible. Jot down below what your answers should be or include. Use your resume as the script to build the answers to these questions.

Tell me your biggest weakness?

_____

_____

_____

_____

_____

_____

Why should we hire you?

_____

_____

_____

_____

_____

_____

Why did you leave your last job?

_____

_____

_____

_____

_____

_____

Where do you see yourself in 5 years?

_____

_____

_____

_____

_____

_____

When did you fail?

_____

_____

_____

_____

_____

_____

When did you succeed?

_____

_____

_____

_____

_____

_____

Do you know how to be part of a team?

_____

_____

_____

_____

_____

_____

Do you have any questions for me?

_____

_____

_____

_____

_____

Let's start with the last question. This is dependent on the interview and what is discussed during the session. It is so important to answer the question no matter what. You have to have a question to ask and you should have this be focused and part of the discussion you had with the interviewer.

So many people let this opportunity pass them by. This is your chance to stand out and to be noticed during the interviewing process by asking a great focused question that helps tie together that you were listening and involved during the interview.

With "Tell me your biggest weakness?" it is time to weave your story and to make it shine. You do not just say a weakness. During my workshops and trainings, I have seen people say, for example, "My biggest weakness is people annoy me."

What do you think about that answer? That answer is not going to cut it or make you look good – it shows that you are maybe throwing shade about the interviewer maybe annoying you. It is important to tell a story about what your biggest weakness is and how you overcame it.

Do not answer this question like the millions who have come before you and say, "I just work too hard." This is not a good answer either.

Try something like this, "I can be a control freak but I have learned through the running of multimillion dollar projects that I have trained them and given my staff and team the lessons so I learned that it is important to trust that training and let go."

So now go back up and see what you think about what you wrote and practice as much as you can.

The next question is, "Why should I hire you." This should dictate and discuss the strengths you have as they apply to the job you are interested in and how you could hit the ground running. The big fear is again that you are "new" but using your other experiences at other jobs or internships to help describe and explain how you can succeed at this role.

Why did you leave your last job should always be answered in a positive way. You should never ever talk badly about previous jobs, coworkers, bosses or anything. Even if your last boss was your mom do not ever say anything negative. If you trash talk your previous jobs or experiences, the assumption will be that you will trash talk them or that you are just a bad apple.

With the question of where do you see yourself in 5 years, you should weave together your strengths and talents and discuss how you can build out your career at the company you are meeting with and hoping to join. Please do not say that you will be taking their job in 5 years. Keep it positive and focused on what you can bring to the company; if you know and understand anything about the company and its products think about how you can clarify and discuss what you could do for the company.

The questions on tell me about when you failed and tell me about when you succeeded these questions can be considered a two for one. Again use your resume to build out your answers and tell your story. Make the story about your failure be one of redemption and how you learned from said failure.

The success story should be about team based successes; do not brag too much make the story be more focused on what you did and how you did it.

Being a part of a team you can discuss group projects, team experiences and how you manage being both a leader and a team member.

All of these stories should be a balance between bragging and telling your story while being engaged and focused on the interviewer. Of course, sometimes you will be interviewed one on one and sometimes you will be taking part in a group interview where there are multiple interviewers or interviewees.

On Group Interviews – Group Interviewees or Group Interviewers

If you are interviewed by more than one interviewer, do the same as you would with one interviewer. Make eye contact, be personable and do not freak out.

Sometimes, you walk in and you freak because instead of just one on one it has become a group setting. Some people are naturally shy and nervous about speaking in front of more than one or two people. Try to work this out in your practice sessions. Learn how to "work" a table of people. Make eye contact with the person asking you the question but then break up your eye contact and look around the room at everyone. Engage people in your discussion and smile normally and naturally.

Other times, when you interview, you will be one of many interviewees sitting in the room. For this situation it is important to stand out in a positive way. You should not give in to yelling over other interviewees or sitting quietly either. You should talk though. Do not sit quietly the whole time. Make sure you try to engage and even think of how you can build off of someone else's comment or thought and be the person who makes the best impression possible.

Always ask for business cards for the interviewer(s) and keep track in your notes to make sure you remember important things about people who you met with – for instance, if one of the interviewers went to your alma mater, you should make a note of it so that you can include it for the thank you note (see Chapter 9 for more on this). Try to have your notes reflect some of the stuff you have discussed with the interviewers to help you build out a personalized letter and to help the interviewer remember you, too.

Remember that even though you will graduate with a job offer with my help from this book that you will be interviewing for the rest of your career. You will maybe stay in your first role for a year or so and then it will be time to move on or maybe something will change and you will need to move on. Keep this book handy and your thoughts and answers to these questions updated. I can almost guarantee you that even if you interview in ten years, some of these questions will still be asked!

Chapter 8:

Media Training Overview

Media training is something I have devised and launched on my blog and also in my workshops and seminars on college and career readiness. It is rare that you will only be interviewed in person today. There are phone interviews, SKYPE based interviews and sometimes a weird hybrid thing where you are interviewed using a one way video to show your abilities on your own.

If you already have created and shared YouTube videos, please review and check the settings on this. Much like in thinking about social media, less is more. You should be focusing on using social media to build your brand and showcase your professionalism not your fun party type stuff.

You really need to be "media" ready and make sure that your message and the essence of who you are and what you can bring to any corporate role.

For phone based interviews, we are removing your ability to connect with the interviewer face to face. We are removing body language and only left with vocal skills. Your voice should be reflective and take over for the lack of body language. Have your voice intonate and be pleasant. Be focused and engaged via phone. Leave pauses and do not be afraid to ask for someone to repeat themselves if you did not hear it well.

In this day and age without real home phones, most of us are using our cell phones for these interviews. Your phone should be someplace where you have full service. You should use a headset so that you can place your phone down and engage in the conversation. Be sure no one is around and going to be calling your name for dinner and/or otherwise making a scene around you. You should be someplace quiet as one of the worst things is to be on an interview via phone and have there be too much background noise so that you cannot hear each other.

Practice with your cell phone videotaping yourself and use SKYPE to practice interviewing and playing it back to see how you come across. It is important to think about where you put your eyes during interviewing via video and SKYPE. It is also important that you know exactly where you will be doing the interview, how quiet it will be around you and removing others from the background of the interviewing location.

Always be fully dressed for the interview; do not be tempted to remain in your pajama bottoms as you might forget and stand up and show everyone your half dressed. Make sure the place where you are recording and using has a normal backdrop – no blown up pictures of Justin Bieber on your wall behind you.

Practice looking into the camera and breaking eye contact only to give a scan of the room of the screen for who is interviewing you. Try to have the names of who is interviewing you via SKYPE in advance but if not, you can use the time during the call to just focus as much as possible and then you can follow up with whoever set up the interview to get the names and contact information of the people who were on the video call.

Try to simulate eye contact and beware what your body language looks like during the video call. Be aware some people have resting mean face so work on your facial expressions and how you look during the interview.

The best way to be comfortable on a media based interview is by being very practiced as an interviewee so knowing how to answer the questions and how to be engaging on an interview.

Remembering that interviewing via a phone call or a video based interview takes away your ability to be present with another person and that most hiring decisions are made based off of someone feeling that you have a relationship to build off of and that you will fit in to the company.

If the interview is being done via a one way video feed, good luck. You will not have another person in the process with you but will just be doing the video on your own. This is hard to do and the best you can have ready is to be comfortable on screen.

For any of these video based interviewing, it is important to be comfortable on video, to know how you react when on your own and being interviewed. So if you have a nervous habit of playing with your hair or picking your nail, beware that you do not do this during the interview.

Practice as much as possible so that you know what you want to say and so that you can be present and personable on the various media. Also keep in mind that once you find your career, you will always be interviewing and you will also be doing video calls and meetings for work, too.

Chapter 9:

What to Do After the Interview

Here is the fun part; in my workshops and seminars when I review the steps to follow after an interview, I definitely see some eye rolls and hear some complaints but I stand by this and I often get a follow up from the students who tell me they did not listen to me at first and failed and then they decided to give my way a try and boom – success!

The point of an interview is to build a relationship. End of story. It is not about getting a job and closing a deal every time. If it were, you would only interview a handful of times in your life and would not have the need to keep interviewing and keep meeting people.

To build these relationships, you have to think about interviewing in a new and exciting way. You have to consider that some of the people you meet, if you feel you are connecting with them it is important to continue that connection in some acceptable way even if you did not get the job or you got the job but turned it down.

A great way to build a relationship is to professionally follow up after the interview with both an email thank you and a Word document thank you letter that is also sent via mail.

80

I know this is considered archaic and old fashioned but it is so important to follow up after the meeting with a personalized letter and note that ties in to the discussion you had with the interviewer.

When I give my workshops, I ask the students if they know how to write a business letter. Everyone says no. It is quite depressing, actually.

My idea is that you use your header from your resume as your letterhead for your letters.

Everything can be left justified from there (except for your name and email and phone number that are in the header).

I am including a template in this book for you to follow. You prepare the letter with the email. The email can be addressed as you were in person together. So this means, if when you met, the interviewer told you, "Hi, I am Joe. Nice to meet you." Then you can address the email to "Dear Joe," The email should be quick and to the point but you cannot send it until the Word document is ready to attach.

Dear Joe,

It was a pleasure meeting with you today to discuss X job at your company. Attached to this email is a thank you letter, which I also sent via US Postal Service.

<Include a sentence or two about the job or what you spoke about.>

I look forward to meeting with you again.

Warmest regards,

Your Name

Cell Phone Number

The business letter format and template information is below. The letter should be addressed to Mr. Smith even if you were calling him "Joe" during the meeting.

Your Address

City, State Zip

DATE

Addressee Name

Title

Company Name

Address

City, State Zip

Dear Mr. X,

First paragraph about how you enjoyed meeting with them on date about x position.

Second paragraph should include a story from your discussion – something about what you discussed and why you are best for the job.

Closing paragraph about looking forward to meeting again about the position/company etc.

Sincerely,

Your Name

By sending the email with the attached letter AND sending the letter via the mail, you are making yourself be in the mind of the interviewer.

If you found you and the interviewer really hit it off and that the conversation was really a potential mentoring session, it is ok to mention in the letter that you would like to connect via LinkedIn or to ask when meeting with the person if it would be ok to connect. If it is ok to connect via LinkedIn, use this relationship to share content and continue to build that mentoring relationship with the person. If they say they do not use LinkedIn or that it is not something they can do, say thank you and leave it alone.

This is a risky thing to do and I would only recommend doing it when you really hit it off with the interviewer. If the person is super impressed by you, they might look for you online via LinkedIn and connect with you.

If not, you can still maintain those business cards and think about if/when you should contact them again. Be careful with this – you do not want to be too much and cross any professional lines but it is a possibility that you can build a true relationship with the interviewers.

If the interviewer tells you to connect with them on LinkedIn and to keep them posted on where you wind up, do this. Do not think someone is just telling you this just to say it. I run this social experiment all of the time. I give out my business cards at workshops and training and tell the students to email me, to connect with me via LinkedIn, to send me their resumes and out of 100 students, only a handful will follow up with me. I think we all consider people do not truly want us to follow up when in reality we do want you to do this. Keep that in mind as you are meeting with people on your career search.

Chapter 10:

Finding Opportunities

The most important thing is to keep an open mind. This can be the whole chapter – keep an open mind.

In keeping an open mind, maintain and build your relationships and your network.

Make sure your social media is on point and that you are using it to build your brand and not your likes. Begin sharing your content, your papers and your work experiences either via LinkedIn or via your own website. Use social media to present yourself as a professional potential career person.

Even if you study marketing and only want to be a marketing person, do not only look for marketing jobs. Keep in mind most graduates wind up working in a field that is not their field and that you might wind up identifying a new niche and/or field that fits you better.

As you build your network and get ready for taking that big step into career from college, always keep in mind that you should ensure everyone knows you are available and looking for a career. You should make sure people know you are flexible, professional and ready for work.

You cannot just find a job by searching online for it. By all means, do submit your resume and cover letter for jobs and personalize the cover letter for the roles you want. However, it is best to build your network and have them be looking for a career FOR you.

By using LinkedIn appropriately as discussed in this book and having your resume and your keywords on point can lead to you getting interviews without having to look for anything, if done really right.

Also consider your friends, family and friends' families. Make sure everyone knows who you are and what you bring to the table. How can you do this? Have an elevator value pitch. I talk about this a lot in terms of how to identify and share your pitch your value statement about who you are and what you are looking for in your career. It is ok to have a wide net that you put out there for multiple different opportunities or paths. The key is that your elevator value pitch highlights and showcases who you are and what you can do.

By being focused, using social media, making sure you build and cultivate your network and using your elevator value pitch, you will definitely be well on your way to getting a job offer and building your career.

Things to keep in mind when moving forward in your path to get a career is to always be professional. Remember that you are young and that there are stereotypes involved with being "young" that include being unprofessional and/or partying too much. Always dress professionally and be on time and focused while at work. Beware people who want to talk too much about the fun times you had during the weekend or who try to pigeonhole you into being considered flaky and/or too "fun".

As you build out your work experiences, you will learn that it is important to balance your work persona and your other persona and how to balance that becomes easier as you continue to build your career.

Chapter 11:

Closing the Deal or Negotiating and Accepting the Offer

If and when you get the job offer you have been waiting for or even you find yourself with multiple job offers or maybe an offer you do not want to have, please consider that you need to be professional in dealing with this step. If you are unsure if you want the job, you might be more willing to negotiate. The rule of thumb is that no one is comfortable negotiating but that it should be done.

With your first job offer, whatever you start your salary history at is what will set the tone for most of your career or at least the first few years. More and more people discuss how important it is to move around in order to continue to grow your salary and options. The idea is that wherever you wind up or whatever you negotiate will set the tone for the next few years.

A piece of advice I always share with my students is about how the world of corporate America works in terms of salaries and career growth. When you are hired, you are hired for a role that maybe existed for decades or is a new role. The role is defined with Human Resources and your management for the department. It is defined in terms of a job description, which might be public on the job listing or might be kept in house and not shared until the person is found for the role.

What you might not ever see is the "ranking" of the position or the "band" of the role. So, some companies use letters, some use numbers. A role of "band 20" might be mid-management at one firm or entry level at another. This "band" or ranking includes salary levels and other potential perks like stock options, bonuses and more. It is important to try to understand where you are in your organization as soon as you can. It might be tough to find this out when interviewing and accepting your first job offer but if you can get and understand this information from day one, you can be that much ahead of anyone else trying to run their careers.

Once the offer is made, you can discuss with Human Resources what the level of the role is and you can try to decipher what the salary bands are although they are less likely to tell you that. If the role you are hired for has a salary band of from $30,000 to $50,000 that means that you cannot be considered for a promotion to the next level until you get closer to the higher band of the salary.

So if you are hired at $30,000, that means you would have to gain $20k in salary raises before you can even be considered moving up the chain of command at your company.

And how does that eventual move happen in your company? For most companies and employees, each year, the performance review is done and it is mostly unpleasant for everyone. Bosses hate doing it, employees hate doing it. Everyone does it anyway.

You have to use the job description to identify and highlight your "goals" for the year – or maybe your management will tell you're your goals. It is important to keep track of how you do with these goals and each year, you will be writing and compiling your statistics in your performance review.

The performance review document is written in the 3rd person and explains the role you filled in the company and details all of the successes you have had. It is important to be able to document this and to build out on the goals given and also to add new things that you took initiative on and ran with, too.

Do the best you can in setting up the job offer, salary and level you are hired at to be ready to continue to grow your career. I recommend my book The Prof's Guide to Entrepreneur-ING: Using Entrepreneurial Skills to Launch Your Own Business or be the Boss of Your Career to be ready to maintain and build your career.

Consider taking the job you are offered and be willing to stick it out for at least a year. It is not as big of a deal as it used to be to show longevity in a role but it would be great to show some results and work hard to remove the "green" off of the perception of being untested in professional environments.

Be professional in picking your job offer. When you say you will work at a company, do not rescind and change your mind unless you really had no choice or something absolutely amazing came up that you just cannot help yourself. Remember until you are processed and in the chair at the job, you do not have a job.

If you are continuing to interview even after accepting a job offer, be prepared for there to be competition and/or something conflicting being offered. You should be honest with any future interviews and tell them you have accepted an offer. It is ok to receive an offer to use it to potentially build out a better offer somewhere else but realize it might backfire on you.

Continue to network and build relationships as a professional. Be willing to reboot – if you have always wanted to be an accountant and then in landing your first job as an accountant, you find yourself miserable every day, be willing to try something new.

Never get "stuck" in a rut or a role where you are unhappy. Be professional and build out relationships by understanding that you should be honest about your shortcomings but focused on always learning and getting better at what you do. It will take time, but eventually, you will be building out your career and hopefully sharing lessons like I am with others to help them take their next steps.

Always focus on where you want to see yourself and how you can grow and continue to build your career and skills.

Build and maintain your network beyond just liking their LinkedIn posts. Share your position and activities as professionally as you can using LinkedIn. If you find yourself new to an industry, read everything you can about the industry. Try to demonstrate that you are a fast learner even if you are struggling. Learn how to ask questions and to be focused on learning on the job to shine. The next chapter will talk more about how to focus on learning to continue growing your career.

Chapter 12:

Building Your Career with Skills and Learning

Never stop learning. This is the crux of being successful and building out a career that goes beyond your first job offer to a successful path of growth and continued success.

Work on skills that can be translated into any industry and/or any type of role. Consider being an entrepreneur and building out other paths that you can use said skills on to always be employed.

Realize that sometimes careers do not go as planned. You can plan and be ready for anything but something else will happen instead. It is like trying to identify risks for a multi-million dollar project – it is rarely one of the risks you thought it would be but if you have a great mitigation plan, you will find something will work and cover the unexpected change.

So continue to learn but shy away from spending tons of money or going into more debt to learn with big time degree programs. Understand that almost everyone today has a bachelor's degree and tons more are getting Master's, MBA's and MS's. Really think hard about if that degree can truly help you and even better if your company will pay for it, then do it.

Try to never stay somewhere where you feel your soul is being crushed. Always have a plan and 2 backup plans on top of that (or as my friend's like to say a backup for your backup). Try to save money so that you have enough saved up to float you if you decide to remove yourself from a bad situation or a bad boss or any other debacle that can come up.

Do not be afraid to hit the reboot button, ever. It is something you might find you need. You maybe did not plan on having kids but wind up with 10 (you never know) so never say "never".

Take the opportunities, take the risks – go for foreign assignments and risky companies to gather and build your skill sets. Focus on what you are learning and how you can give back and share the knowledge. Sign up to speak at your alma mater or attend a networking event that they offer for students.

See if you can give back to your high school or better yet identify a school that has lots of need and go there. Instead of giving money, give your time. By teaching and sharing your lessons, you will learn more than any teacher (including I) can teach you.

Be inspired and inspiring – try to balance it all and then realize how hard it can be to balance the house, the family, the career. Enjoy the challenge and when it is no longer fun, be ready to find something else to learn from and move forward in doing.

Always take time to read. Read for fun and read for work. Start to write – draft out some blog posts about your career or about what you wish you knew when you were younger and share it. Be brave enough to share it.

When you make a mistake (and you will) just admit it and move on. If you cannot move on (if it was a real bad mistake), suck it up and deal with the fall out. Be honest. Be focused.

Keep moving forward and building out the career you want – if you always dreamed of being CEO and then get close to your dream and realize it was all a mistake then be brave enough to pull the plug and try something different. As much as people tell you to do what you love and the money will come it can actually come true if you truly know what you love and can figure out a way to help others with it and then you can build that career around that dream.

I hope you decide to continue to learn with me on my blog, my workshops, training programs and more. Consider me a mentor and someone who is interested in learning with you on how you succeed and how you take my lessons and apply them to your first job and your whole career.

In Closing:

Thank you so much for reading this book! Please feel free to contact me with any questions or concerns at www.thenextstep1234.com or follow me for more advice and tips on Twitter and Instagram @thenext_step123.

This book is based off of over 13 years' experience as an educator at the college level. The tips and advice written are applicable to your life.

I truly hope you decide to continue to learn from me and that you reach out to me with any questions via my website or email lisa@thenextstep1234.com.

If there is anything this edition did not address that you think future editions should, please let me know. If you did not agree with something or think I need to add more to included topics, let me know that, too. Writing is something you do alone but you want to have people who read it impacted and/or provide feedback so please feel free to let me know what you think!

Happy Hunting!

Previously published books by Lisa Vento Nielsen

The Prof's Guide to Entrepreneur-ing – Using Entrepreneurial Skills to Launch Your Own Business or be the Boss of Your Career

The Book on College Readiness The Prof's Guide to Surviving High School and Kicking Butt in College *(First in a series on College & Career Readiness)*

Books in progress by Lisa Vento Nielsen:

The Prof's Guide to Entrepreneur-ing: Going from 0toLaunch – Everything you need to know to be an entrepreneur as of today

How to Blog Like a Pro-Fessor

Made in the USA
Coppell, TX
17 August 2021